DATE DUE

GAYLORD			PRINTED IN U.S.A.

D0849372

21st
Century
Skills Library

COOL STEM CAREERS

EPIDEMIOLOGIST

NEL YOMTOV

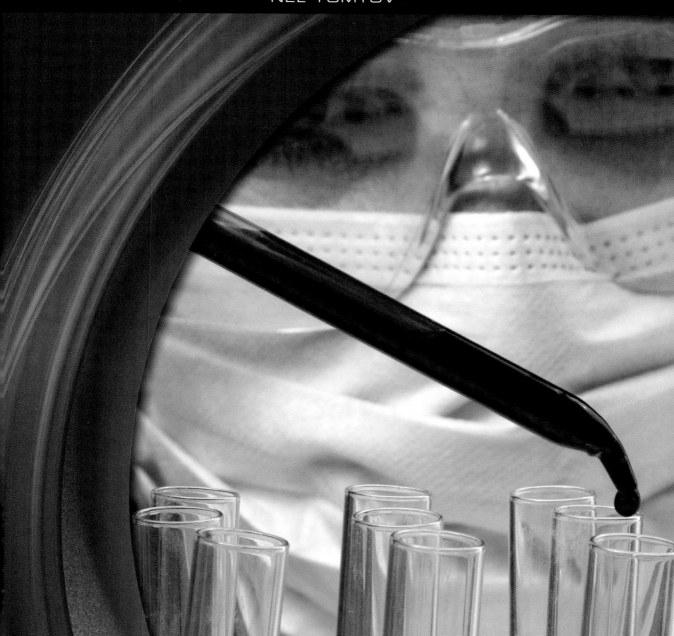

Published in the United States of America by
Cherry Lake Publishing, Ann Arbor, Michigan
www.cherrylakepublishing.com

Content Adviser
Wendy G. Lane, MD, MPH, Associate Director, Preventive Medicine Residency
Program; Assistant Professor, Department of Epidemiology and Public Health and
Department of Pediatrics, University of Maryland School of Medicine, Baltimore,
Maryland

Photo Credits: Cover and pages 1 and 18, ©Rob Byron/Shutterstock, Inc.;
page 4, ©AP Photo/Chris Carlson; page 6, ©Rmarmion/Dreamstime.com; page 8,
©Elena Elisseeva/Shutterstock, Inc.; page 11, ©Hinochika/Shutterstock, Inc.; page 12,
©Mary Evans Picture Library/Alamy; page 16, ©Andre Blais/Shutterstock, Inc.;
page 20, ©Lisa S./Shutterstock, Inc.; page 22, ©AP Photo/Kevork Djansezian; page 24,
©CandyBox Images/Shutterstock, Inc.; page 26, ©Fotokostic/Shutterstock, Inc.

Library of Congress Cataloging-in-Publication Data
Yomtov, Nelson.
  Epidemiologist / by Nel Yomtov.
      p. cm.—(21st century skills library) (Cool STEM careers)
  Audience: Grade 4 to 6.
  Includes bibliographical references and index.
  ISBN 978-1-62431-007-2 (lib. bdg.) — ISBN 978-1-62431-031-7 (pbk.) —
ISBN 978-1-62431-055-3 (e-book)
  1. Epidemiologists—Juvenile literature. 2. Epidemiology—Vocational guidance—
Juvenile literature. I. Title.
  RA653.5.Y65 2013
  614.4—dc23   2012034721

Cherry Lake Publishing would like to acknowledge
the work of The Partnership for 21st Century Skills.
Please visit *www.21stcenturyskills.org* for more information.

Printed in the United States of America
Corporate Graphics Inc.
January 2013
CLFA11

<cept...

COOL STEM CAREERS

TABLE OF CONTENTS

EPIDEMIOLOGIST

CHAPTER ONE
DISEASE HUNTERS

Andrew was puzzled as he looked out his kitchen window one night. A large vehicle was driving slowly down his block. "What's that truck doing?" he asked his father.

Trucks with sprayers help prevent the spread of disease-carrying insects.

Andrew's dad came to the window for a closer look. "See that sprayer mounted on the back of the truck? It's shooting a fine chemical mist into the air," he replied.

"What's the chemical for?" Andrew asked. "Is there something wrong with the air in our neighborhood?"

"The chemical is used to kill mosquitoes that might carry the West Nile **virus**. That can lead to a serious illness."

"Who figured out that such a small insect could be dangerous to people?" Andrew asked.

"Lots of that type of work is done by scientists and researchers called **epidemiologists**," replied Andrew's dad. "They figure out what causes certain diseases and then inform people how to prevent them."

"Sounds like a cool job," said Andrew. "I'd sure like to be a disease hunter!"

■ ■ ■

Epidemiology is the study of the causes, occurrences, and control of disease and other public health problems in populations, or groups of people. When we think of medicine, we usually think of doctors and nurses who deal with health and disease in individuals. Epidemiologists, however, identify the nature of diseases and why groups of people get them.

Epidemiologists work to limit disability, injury, and death in a population. The word *epidemiology* comes from several

Greek words. *Epi* means "on," *demos* means "the common people" or "population," and *logy* means "study." Combining these terms tells us that epidemiology is the study of things that affect the common people.

Epidemiologists are often called medical detectives. They search for clues, investigate evidence, and arrive at conclusions. Instead of tracking down criminals, however, they study areas that relate to public health. One of these areas is the outbreak of **epidemics**. An epidemic is an **infectious**

Epidemiologists study diseases to find new cures and ways of preventing illness.

disease that appears in a large number of people at the same time. There have been epidemics of diseases such as AIDS, whooping cough, and measles.

Tiny forms of life called organisms cause many of the diseases that epidemiologists study. These organisms include viruses, **bacteria**, and **parasites**. They may spread from person to person or from insects to people. They might travel through the air we breathe, the food we eat, the water we drink or bathe in, or the fluids in our bodies. Epidemiologists must search for the clues that tell them the cause of the epidemic disease like detectives at the scene of a crime. They try to learn how it spreads through the population.

Infectious diseases are not the only illnesses that epidemiologists investigate, however. These medical detectives examine chronic diseases such as cancer, arthritis, diabetes, and even back pain. They also study illnesses that result from environmental factors, or a person's surroundings. Examples are allergies and birth defects.

Some epidemiologists research health conditions related to a person's **genetics**. Others study mental illness or the effects of nutrition on health. Epidemiologists have also made great strides in improving health by preventing injuries. For example, they have studied injuries to children in car crashes. Their findings have helped design car seats that better protect young passengers. Epidemiologists have also investigated scald burns in children. This has led to new laws that set a maximum temperature for home hot-water heaters. In other words, epidemiologists investigate just about anything that relates to the causes and patterns of diseases and disabilities. They use their research to help prevent or control these issues.

Epidemiologists make important contributions to public health on local, national, and worldwide levels. They share their findings with governments, health care providers, and communities. Their research evaluates community health

Studies conducted by epidemiologists have proven that bicycle helmets can prevent head injuries.

problems and offers solutions. Using this valuable data, communities develop programs to control or prevent the causes of the problems. One example is spraying neighborhoods to prevent the spread of the West Nile virus. Communities have also established antismoking programs and passed laws that require bike riders to wear helmets.

LEARNING & INNOVATION SKILLS

Stacie Neff is an epidemiologist at the Centers for Disease Control and Prevention (CDC) in Fort Collins, Colorado. It's a job that keeps her on her toes. "One day I may work on a big project surveying diseases on a national level, and the next, I might be across the country somewhere working 16-hour days on a disease outbreak," explains Neff. One summer, Neff and her team were called to Louisiana. They needed to investigate an outbreak of the West Nile virus. She and her team worked around the clock. They examined patients, took blood samples, and analyzed the data they collected from 196 patients. Such information helps the scientists better understand the virus, and how it can be treated and controlled.

Epidemiologists have made many lifesaving discoveries over the years. They helped find ways to stop the spread of diseases such as **cholera** and measles. They established links between smoking and cancer. They showed that eating shellfish can sometimes be harmful to pregnant women. Epidemiologists helped identify the virus that causes the deadly severe acute respiratory syndrome (SARS), which first appeared in China in 2002. They discovered that drivers who use cell phones while driving increase their chances of becoming involved in a car accident.

This small sampling of epidemiological accomplishments shows how the work of these researchers affects our daily lives. Their recommendations help governments and public health organizations develop and carry out programs that improve life for everyone. Although epidemiologists study the health of a population, their findings affect each of us in a very personal way.

Epidemiology is a booming field of study with many career opportunities. The field is growing in size and importance each year. The number of epidemiologists worldwide and the number of training programs in colleges and universities have increased rapidly. This energetic growth has come mainly in the last 50 years. But the development of epidemiology dates back almost 400 years. Since that time, epidemiologists have made many startling and significant discoveries.

Some people wear masks in public during epidemics to help protect against infection.

CHAPTER TWO
PIONEERS OF EPIDEMIOLOGY

The slow, steady development of epidemiology came from many fields, including medicine, **sociology**, and **statistics**. However, it was not until the 19th century that epidemiology blossomed into its own field.

The plague first swept through Europe in the 14th century.

John Graunt was a British shopkeeper who lived in the 1600s. He is often called the world's first epidemiologist. Graunt analyzed lists of deaths in London, England, during an outbreak of the bubonic plague. The plague, or Black Death, caused devastating epidemics in the 1300s and later. Graunt noted that the most common causes of death in London in the 1600s were the Black Death, old age, a highly contagious illness called smallpox, and gum disease. He also discovered that some of the most commonly feared causes of death, such as suicide and starvation, were rare. Graunt's system of reporting deaths to local officials is a forerunner for the system used in the United States today.

The next major milestone in the history of epidemiology took place not in a heavily populated city but on the high seas. James Lind was a surgeon in the British navy in the 1700s. Lind observed that many sailors suffered from scurvy, a common disease and cause of death at the time. Scurvy causes swollen, bleeding gums and severe exhaustion.

Lind rejected the traditional belief that scurvy was a genetic or infectious disease. He believed its cause was poor diet. While sailing on the HMS *Salisbury* in 1747, Lind decided to test his belief. He split 12 sick sailors into six groups of two. He then fed them the same diet except each group was given a different item to eat or drink. For example, one group drank vinegar three times a day. Another group drank seawater. A third group ate citrus fruits—two oranges and one lemon—every day.

After four weeks, Lind reported that "the most sudden and visible good effects were perceived from the use of the oranges and lemons." Lind had discovered that scurvy was caused by a lack of vitamin C, which is found in citrus fruits. He conducted similar experiments on other ships and voyages. The results always supported his conclusions. It was 40 years before the British navy started serving citrus fruits to its sailors. But when it finally did, scurvy was eliminated within several years.

A doctor named John Snow is often called the father of modern epidemiology for his work combating an outbreak of cholera in 19th-century London. In the 1830s, London was a filthy city. Poor people lived in unsanitary conditions. Rotting garbage littered the streets. Human and animal waste was channeled into the river Thames, the source of London's drinking, cooking, and washing water. By 1832, a cholera epidemic had erupted in the city. Dozens of people were dying each day. No one knew why.

Snow believed that dirty water was causing the rapid spread of cholera. In 1848, he began gathering records of cholera deaths. He also learned about the companies that supplied water to the city's different neighborhoods. When another outbreak erupted in central London in August and September 1854, he intensified his research. He traveled door-to-door conducting interviews in neighborhoods where people were dying of the disease. He also questioned families of cholera victims about where they got their water.

LIFE & CAREER SKILLS

Epidemiologists are particularly interested in identifying and studying the so-called index case. An index case is the first instance of a condition or disease to be identified in a population. In most outbreaks of an infectious disease, the index case is the one that introduced the disease into the population. Identifying the index case can provide clues about the origins of the outbreak, how it spread, and whether the disease could spread further. The index case is sometimes referred to as patient zero. This is particularly true when epidemiologists wish to protect an individual's identity.

Finally, at a city meeting in September 1854, Snow announced to town leaders that the water from a specific public pump was the cause of the problem. He convinced officials to close down the pump. Afterwards, the number of cholera cases decreased, and the epidemic eased in that part of London. His work saved the lives of thousands of Londoners.

Today, we know that bacteria that can live in water for long periods cause cholera.

Another important event in the history of epidemiology took place in 1950. British researchers Richard Doll and Austin Bradford Hill decided to conduct a study on the link between smoking and lung cancer. They had noticed a huge increase in deaths from lung cancer in England and Wales

Epidemiologists have proven that smoking can cause deadly diseases.

after World War I (1914–1918). The epidemiologists interviewed about 700 people with lung cancer and asked them questions about their smoking habits. Had they ever smoked during their lives? If so, at what ages did they start? How much did they smoke? Did they inhale?

Doll and Hill found that smoking was far more common among lung cancer patients than among noncancer patients. Although they did not know how tobacco caused cancer, they concluded that smoking was a contributing factor. Studies by other researchers in the 1950s supported their findings. In a later study with tens of thousands of subjects, Doll and Hill found similar results.

After reviewing the work of Doll and Hill, and other epidemiologists, U.S. surgeon general Luther L. Terry issued a report in 1964 outlining the hazards of smoking. The report also pointed to the connections between smoking and **emphysema** and heart disease. According to Terry, the report "hit the country like a bombshell." The work of Doll, Hill, and others led to public health efforts to help people quit smoking. Their work also led to the outlawing of smoking in many public places, including restaurants, airplanes, and offices.

As the stories of these pioneers in epidemiology show, the work of a medical detective is challenging and highly rewarding. After all, what is more satisfying than saving lives?

CHAPTER THREE
DIGGING FOR ANSWERS

In their role as medical detectives, epidemiologists investigate epidemics to answer important questions: What causes a specific disease? Where is the disease most likely to break out?

Testing blood samples can provide epidemiologists with helpful information about diseases.

What traits and behaviors do its victims have in common? How can other outbreaks be prevented?

To answer these questions, epidemiologists perform a wide variety of duties. Each duty requires attention to detail and accuracy. Some duties include:

- Collecting and analyzing data
- Examining factors that might put people at risk for illness, such as their race, age, gender, genetics, behaviors, and surroundings
- Designing research studies and conducting research
- Sharing information with other researchers and public health officials
- Writing reports and articles
- Developing and testing theories about what causes disease and how it spreads
- Creating plans to stop the spread of disease

In the first part of an epidemic investigation, epidemiologists gather data. They write questionnaires and conduct interviews about the origin of the outbreak, injury, or illness, and its victims. They may collect biological samples, such as blood, saliva, or skin. Laboratories test these samples to determine causes of the disease and people's response to the infection. After analyzing the data, epidemiologists then develop a strategy to control and prevent other outbreaks.

Epidemiologists often share their findings with government officials. Together they create strategies to inform the public of health risks. They also establish procedures to control and prevent the spread of the disease. Then, they set up programs to monitor the population most at risk.

Epidemiologists perform their work in many settings. The most common are medical, academic, laboratory, or government facilities. Medical settings include hospitals and other health care sites. Academic settings are most often colleges

Epidemiologists use specialized equipment to help them study diseases and potential cures.

and universities. Research laboratories can be found at drug companies, medical schools, and colleges and universities. Local, state, and federal governments employ about 50 percent of the epidemiologists in the United States. These scientists often work in public health departments.

One of the largest government employers of epidemiologists is the U.S. Department of Health and Human Services. This federal agency is responsible for protecting the health of all Americans. The department runs more than 300 different agencies. These include the Centers for Disease Control and Prevention (CDC), the National Institutes of Health (NIH), and the U.S. Food and Drug Administration (FDA).

21ST CENTURY CONTENT

In the 21st century, epidemiologists specializing in genetics are on the cutting edge of the field. They study how genetic factors determine health and disease in families and large populations. Many job opportunities are opening up for these epidemiologists to uncover links between genetic factors and environmental factors, and how they relate to the cause and spread of disease.

Based in Atlanta, Georgia, the CDC employs a large staff of epidemiologists who monitor public health and conduct research on the spread of and prevention of disease. CDC epidemiologists travel all over the world to investigate epidemics such as AIDS, influenza, and SARS. They also investigate the causes of chronic illnesses such as asthma and diabetes. Many epidemiologists begin their careers with the CDC's Epidemic Intelligence Service (EIS), a two-year on-the-job training program.

Food and Drug Administration scientists work to ensure that the food we eat will not harm us.

The NIH, located in Bethesda, Maryland, is the federal government's medical research agency. Its mission is to develop techniques and programs that will improve health worldwide. The NIH has helped reduce the occurrence of cholera in developing countries. NIH scientists have also worked on drugs to treat cancer and help prevent it from coming back. Researchers and epidemiologists at the NIH have discovered new treatments to control heart attacks and certain types of mental illness, as well.

Also headquartered in Maryland is the FDA. This agency tests, approves, and sets safety standards for foods and drugs in the United States. Its epidemiologists review studies evaluating drugs to determine whether they are safe and effective. They help decide which drugs should be approved for treatment of illness or disease.

Many epidemiologists work for international health agencies, such as the World Health Organization (WHO). WHO is the public health agency of the United Nations. It directs and coordinates health-related issues around the world. WHO's vaccination campaigns played a significant role in eliminating smallpox worldwide by the 1970s. Today, WHO conducts research and employs preventive measures for diseases such as AIDS, malaria, and tuberculosis. It also focuses on global issues related to nutrition, aging, alcohol abuse, and air and water quality.

CHAPTER FOUR

A CAREER AS AN EPIDEMIOLOGIST

Becoming an epidemiologist requires planning, training, and education—and the right personal characteristics. You will need at least a master's degree in epidemiology

Epidemiology students learn about the inner workings of the human body.

from a school of public health. This one- or two-year program teaches basic skills in epidemiology. To enter a master's program requires a degree from a four-year college or university. Master's programs may require completion of courses in biology, other sciences, and statistics.

The most common master's degrees available in epidemiology are master of science (MS), master of health science (MHS), and master of public health (MPH). Some epidemiologists have received more extensive training in epidemiology and in designing and conducting research studies. This longer training may lead to a doctorate degree. Such degrees include doctor of science (ScD), doctor of public health (DrPH), or doctor of philosophy (PhD). Some epidemiologists have additional training in nursing, medicine, veterinary medicine, or pharmacy.

In a master's degree program, you will learn how to apply statistics to the study of health and disease, known as biostatistics. You will also learn how to design, conduct, and analyze research studies. Typical courses include laboratory and field research methods, genetics and human disease, and control of infectious diseases.

Once you have gained a basic understanding of epidemiology, you choose your specialty within the field. Some options include environmental health, chronic disease, and women's health. Others choose injury, child health, or drug and alcohol abuse.

Successful medical detectives have a strong interest in the world around them. They also have a passion for making new, exciting discoveries. Having a curious mind and solid critical-thinking and problem-solving skills are essential tools for an epidemiologist. Excellent writing skills will help you write research reports, journal articles, and proposals that request funding for research. Oral presentations to public officials, the media, and the public are often part of an epidemiologist's responsibilities. Because of this, solid verbal skills are a big plus.

You might wonder what you can expect to earn once you have all the necessary academic credentials. In 2010, epidemiologists in the United States earned an average of about $63,000 per year. The lowest earners averaged about $42,000.

It is important for epidemiologists to develop their research and writing skills.

Top earners averaged roughly $98,000. Earnings depend on where you work, your qualifications, and your amount of experience.

LIFE & CAREER SKILLS

The future looks promising for those interested in a career as an epidemiologist. Jobs in the field are estimated to increase by about 25 percent from 2010 to 2020. The boom in the health care industry will create many job opportunities. Researchers who can provide critical information to governments, health agencies, and communities dealing with epidemics will be in high demand. Experts believe that the rise of international travel will increase disease transmission and outbreaks of epidemics worldwide. Treating these illnesses should result in employment opportunities.

Epidemiologists working at drug and manufacturing companies are the highest earners. They average about $93,000 annually. They are followed by hospital epidemiologists working on the local, state, and private level. These scientists typically earn about $73,000 a year. Epidemiologists working in scientific research and development services average $67,000 a year.

Government epidemiologist jobs usually come with excellent benefits. People in these jobs receive paid holidays, sick leave, retirement benefits and pensions, medical benefits, and life insurance. In the private sector, epidemiologists working full-time are typically provided with similar benefits including medical insurance, paid vacations and holidays, and retirement plans.

So how do you begin your exciting journey to become an epidemiologist? To start, take as many science and math courses as you can to help you build a strong foundation. It is never too early, or too late, for junior or senior high school students to contact epidemiology programs that interest them. Ask about their application requirements and for any suggestions to help you get a head start on your career path.

Science camps and precollege summer programs at colleges and universities are also worth investigating. There are many internships and other programs for students interested in science and math. Scholarships are often available if there is need.

Epidemiologists make a difference in our lives. They improve public health and work to ensure the safety and well-being of people throughout the world. Their work is stimulating and challenging, with a wide variety of duties and responsibilities. In addition, numerous jobs in this field offer the opportunity for national and international travel, which appeals to many young people.

The road to becoming a medical detective requires years of education, hard work, and dedication. But for most, the satisfaction of helping people and being part of a well-respected and admired profession is well worth the effort. Are you up to the challenge?

SOME WELL-KNOWN EPIDEMIOLOGISTS

William Farr (1807–1883), a British epidemiologist, was one of the founders of the field of medical statistics. He was able to describe the state of Britain's public health by making calculations based on birth, marriage, and death data and apply that knowledge to preventing and controlling disease there.

John Graunt (1620–1674) is often considered the first epidemiologist and statistician. His work *Natural and Political Observations Made Upon the Bills of Mortality* was published in 1662. It was a reporting of causes of death in London over the previous century. Graunt identified the most common causes of death. He also determined that some diseases affected a similar number of people every year, while others varied over time.

Austin Bradford Hill (1897–1991) and Richard Doll (1912–2005) conducted a study in 1950 on smoking and lung cancer. The study found that a higher percentage of lung cancer patients than noncancer patients were smokers. In 1951, the two British epidemiologists began another study. It eventually showed that smoking causes not only lung cancer but also heart disease and a variety of circulatory system diseases.

James Lind (1716–1794) was a surgeon in the British navy. He conducted one of the earliest studies on the treatment of scurvy. Lind discovered that citrus fruits, such as oranges and lemons, prevented scurvy.

John Snow (1813–1858) was an English doctor who is considered the father of modern epidemiology. He collected records of cholera deaths. He noted that the water supply in certain parts of London came from the sewage-filled river Thames. Snow concluded that dirty water was the cause of the deadly disease.

GLOSSARY

bacteria (bak-TIHR-ee-uh) tiny living organisms that sometimes cause disease

cholera (KAH-lur-uh) a serious infectious disease caused by a bacteria in contaminated food and water and marked by severe vomiting and diarrhea

emphysema (ehm-fuh-ZEE-muh) a disease that results in a severe loss of breathing ability

epidemics (ep-uh-DEM-iks) infectious diseases present in a large number of people at the same time

epidemiologists (eh-puh-dee-mee-AH-luh-jists) people who study the causes, occurrences, and control of disease and other public health problems in a population

genetics (juh-NET-iks) specific characteristics that are passed from parents to offspring

infectious (in-FEK-shuhs) caused by or spread by bacteria or viruses

parasites (PAYR-uh-sites) plants or animals that live on or inside another plant or animal

sociology (soh-see-OL-uh-jee) the study of the ways people live together in societies

statistics (stuh-TISS-tiks) the branch of mathematics related to the collection and analysis of numbers, facts, or other information

virus (VYE-ruhss) a tiny organism that can cause disease; the disease cause by a virus

FOR MORE INFORMATION

BOOKS

Emmer, Richard, Jr. *Virus Hunter*. Philadelphia: Chelsea House, 2006.

Friedlander, Mark P. *Outbreak: Disease Detectives at Work*. Minneapolis: Twenty-First Century Books, 2009.

Gray, Susan Heinrichs. *Disease Control*. Ann Arbor, MI: Cherry Lake Publishing, 2009.

WEB SITES

Centers for Disease Control and Prevention: BAM! (Body and Mind!)
www.bam.gov/sub_diseases/diseases_detectives_2.html
Learn the basics of epidemiology and read an interview with an epidemiologist from the Centers for Disease Control and Prevention (CDC).

Centers for Disease Control and Prevention— Operation: Infection Detection
www.bam.gov/sub_diseases/westNile.swf
Join an epidemiologist in tracking down an outbreak of an unknown disease.

John Hopkins University Center for Talented Youth
www.cogito.org
Review details about internships and summer programs for students interested in science and math.

INDEX

ABOUT THE AUTHOR

Nel Yomtov is an award-winning author of nonfiction books and graphic novels for young readers. He lives in the New York City area.